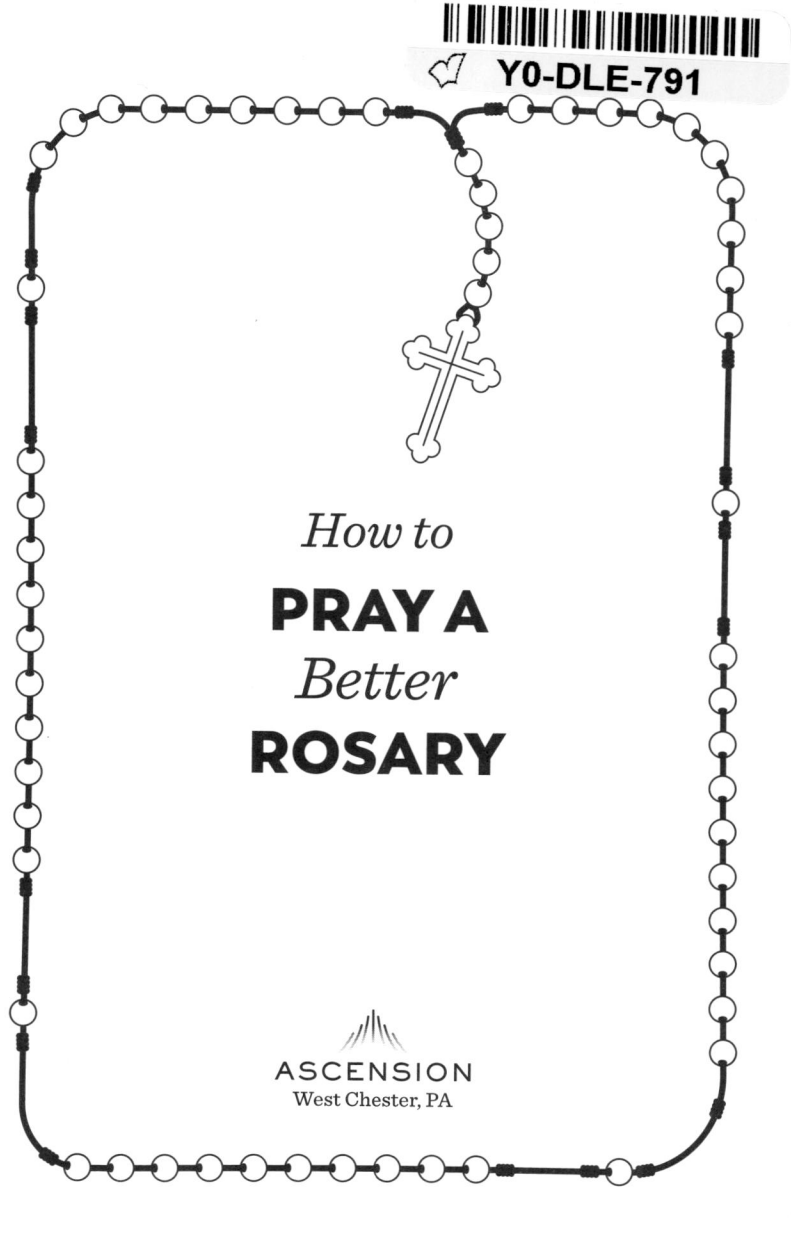

How to
PRAY A *Better* **ROSARY**

ASCENSION
West Chester, PA

Litany of Loreto © 2024 *Amministrazione del Patrimonio della Santa Sede Apostolica and Dicastero per la Comunicazione, Libreria Editrice Vaticana, Città del Vaticano.* All rights reserved.

© 2024 Ascension Publishing Group, LLC. All rights reserved.

With the exception of short excerpts used in articles and critical reviews, no part of this work may be reproduced, transmitted, or stored in any form whatsoever, printed or electronic, without the prior written permission of the publisher.

Excerpts from the English translation of the *Catechism of the Catholic Church* for use in the United States of America © 1994 United States Catholic Conference, Inc.–Libreria Editrice Vaticana. Used with permission. English translation of the *Catechism of the Catholic Church: Modifications from the Editio Typica* © 1997 United States Conference of Catholic Bishops–Libreria Editrice Vaticana.

Scripture quotations are from the Revised Standard Version of the Bible–Second Catholic Edition (Ignatius Edition) copyright © 2006 National Council of the Churches of Christ in the United States of America. Used by permission. All rights reserved.

Ascension
PO Box 1990
West Chester, PA 19380
1-800-376-0520
ascensionpress.com

Cover and interior design: Teresa Ranck

Printed in USA

24 25 26 27 28 5 4 3 2 1

ISBN 979-8-892760-32-4

CONTENTS

How to Pray the Rosary 5
   Prayers of the Rosary 7
   Mysteries of the Rosary 9

How to Pray a Better Rosary 19
   Rosary Fundamentals 20
   From Repetition to Relationship 23
   Litany of the Sacred Heart 25
   Litany of Loreto 30
   Biblical Roots of the Rosary 34
   Our Father 36
   Hail Mary 37
   Glory Be 38
   The Mysteries of the Rosary in Scripture .. 40
   Putting It All Together 45

A Prayer Plan 49
   The Rosary in a Year Prayer Plan 50
   Pray with Us 51

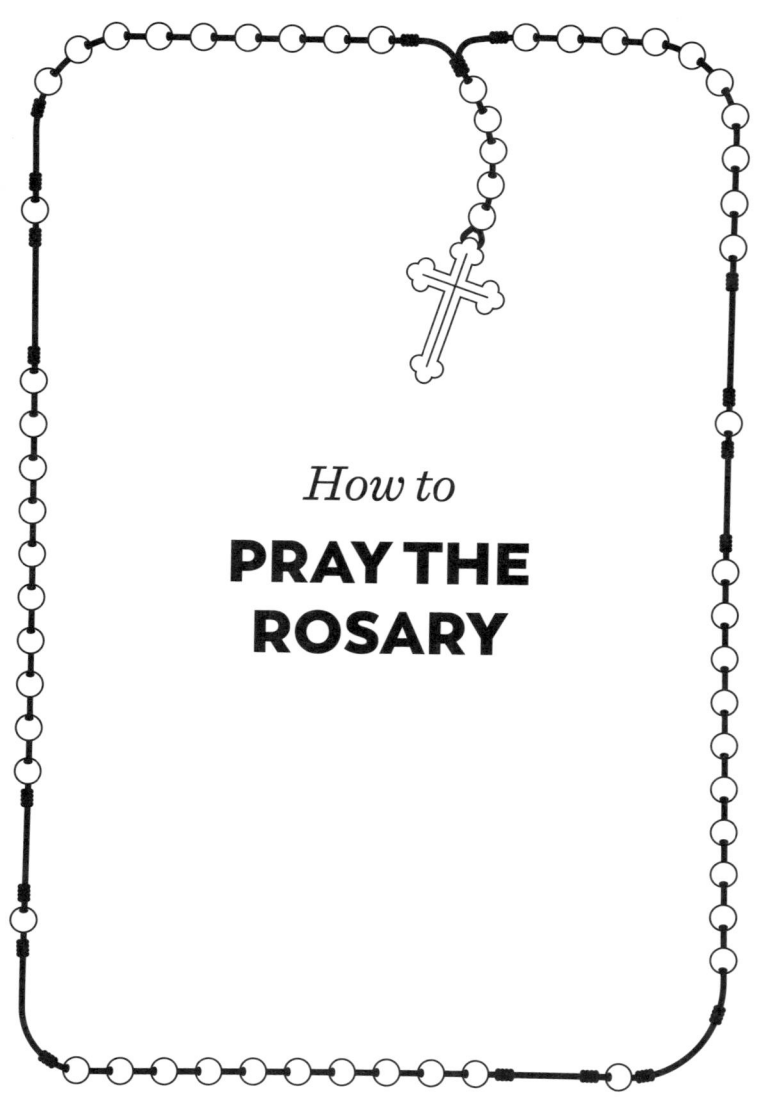

How to PRAY THE ROSARY

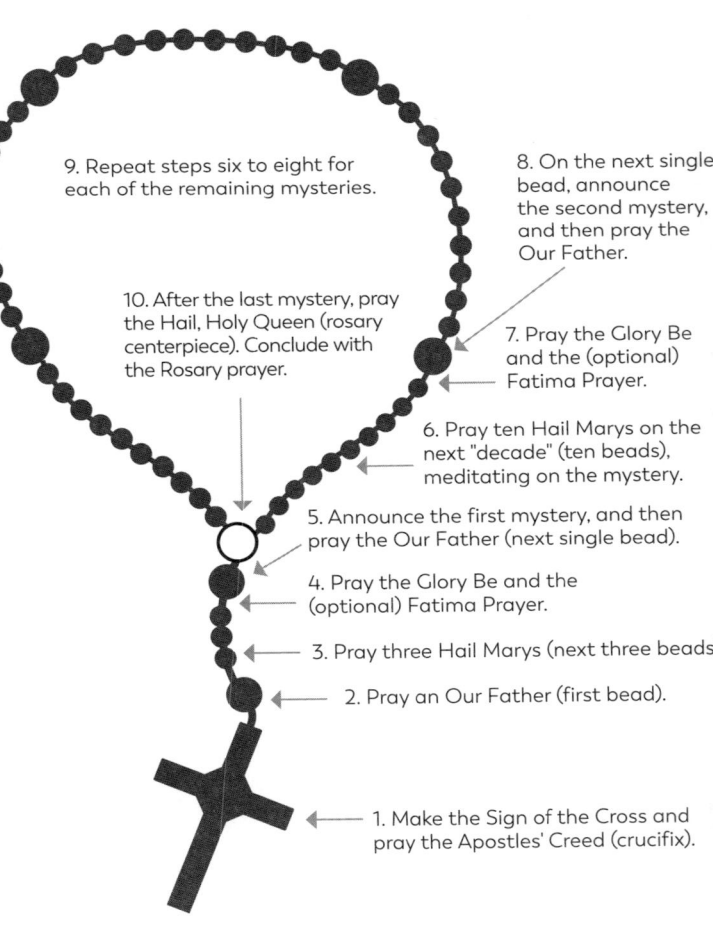

Prayers of the Rosary

APOSTLES' CREED

I believe in God, the Father almighty, Creator of heaven and earth, and in Jesus Christ, his only Son, our Lord, who was conceived by the Holy Spirit, born of the Virgin Mary, suffered under Pontius Pilate, was crucified, died and was buried; he descended to hell; on the third day he rose again from the dead; he ascended into heaven, and is seated at the right hand of God the Father almighty; from there he will come to judge the living and the dead. I believe in the Holy Spirit, the holy catholic Church, the communion of saints, the forgiveness of sins, the resurrection of the body, and life everlasting. Amen.

OUR FATHER

Our Father who art in heaven, hallowed be thy name. Thy kingdom come. Thy will be done on earth, as it is in heaven. Give us this day our daily bread, and forgive us our trespasses, as we forgive those who trespass against us, and lead us not into temptation, but deliver us from evil. Amen.

HAIL MARY

Hail Mary, full of grace, the Lord is with thee. Blessed art thou among women, and blessed is the fruit of thy womb, Jesus. Holy Mary, Mother of God, pray for us sinners, now and at the hour of our death. Amen.

GLORY BE

Glory be to the Father, and to the Son, and to the Holy Spirit, as it was in the beginning, is now, and ever shall be, world without end. Amen.

FATIMA PRAYER

O my Jesus, forgive us our sins, save us from the fires of hell, and lead all souls to heaven, especially those in most need of thy mercy.

HAIL, HOLY QUEEN

Hail, Holy Queen, Mother of mercy, our life, our sweetness, and our hope. To thee do we cry, poor banished children of Eve; to thee do we send up our sighs, mourning and weeping in this valley of tears. Turn, then, most gracious advocate, thine eyes of mercy toward us, and after this, our exile, show unto us the blessed fruit of thy womb, Jesus. O clement, O loving, O sweet Virgin Mary.

ROSARY PRAYER

God, whose only begotten Son, by his life, death, and resurrection, has purchased for us the rewards of eternal life, grant, we beseech thee, that meditating upon these mysteries of the Most Holy Rosary of the Blessed Virgin Mary, we may imitate what they contain and obtain what they promise, through the same Christ our Lord. Amen.

PRAYER TO ST. MICHAEL THE ARCHANGEL

(Note: This beautiful prayer is not part of the Rosary, but it is sometimes prayed at the conclusion of the Rosary.)

St. Michael the Archangel, defend us in battle, be our protection against the wickedness and snares of the Devil. May God rebuke him, we humbly pray, and do thou, O Prince of the Heavenly Host, by the power of God, cast into hell Satan and all the evil spirits, who prowl throughout the world seeking the ruin of souls. Amen.

Mysteries of the Rosary

WHEN TO PRAY EACH SET OF MYSTERIES

- **Sundays:** glorious mysteries*
- **Mondays:** joyful mysteries
- **Tuesdays:** sorrowful mysteries
- **Wednesdays:** glorious mysteries
- **Thursdays:** luminous mysteries
- **Fridays:** sorrowful mysteries
- **Saturdays:** joyful mysteries

Optionally, the joyful mysteries may be prayed on Sundays in Advent, and the sorrowful mysteries may be prayed on Sundays in Lent.

Joyful Mysteries

THE ANNUNCIATION

We pray for a humble heart.[1]

Scripture: Luke 1:26–38

Mary is visited by the archangel Gabriel, who tells her God's plan for her to become the mother of our Savior, Jesus Christ, and she says yes with all her heart.

THE VISITATION

We pray for a charitable heart.

Scripture: Luke 1:39–56

Filled with the Holy Spirit, Mary travels to see her cousin Elizabeth, who joyfully acknowledges Mary as blessed, affirming the divinity of the unborn Jesus.

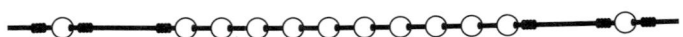

THE NATIVITY

We pray for a heart poor in spirit.

Scripture: Luke 2:1–20

Mary gives birth to Jesus, the Son of God made man, laying him in a simple manger in Bethlehem as angels and shepherds glorify God.

THE PRESENTATION OF JESUS IN THE TEMPLE

We pray for a pure heart.

Scripture: Luke 2:22–39

Mary and Joseph present the infant Jesus in the Temple, where Simeon proclaims that Jesus is the long-awaited Messiah.

THE FINDING OF JESUS IN THE TEMPLE

We pray for conversion of heart.

Scripture: Luke 2:41–52

After searching for Jesus for three days, Mary and Joseph find him in the Temple, his Father's house, where he is talking with great understanding to the teachers.

---

1. Gifts we pray for in the joyful, sorrowful, and glorious mysteries are adapted from *Le Secret Amirable du Très Saint Rosaire* by St. Louis-Marie Grignion de Montfort.

Luminous Mysteries

THE BAPTISM OF JESUS

We pray for a heart faithful to our baptismal vows.

Scripture: Matthew 3:13–17

As Jesus begins his ministry, baptized by John the Baptist, the Holy Spirit descends upon him with the appearance of a dove, and the voice of the heavenly Father declares him beloved.

THE WEDDING AT CANA

We pray for a heart ready to do God's will.

Scripture: John 2:1–12

Mary asks Jesus to perform his first miracle, turning water into wine, which reveals Jesus' power and the importance of Mary's role in leading others to her son.

THE PROCLAMATION OF THE KINGDOM AND THE CALL TO CONVERSION

We pray for a heart filled with faith.

Scripture: Mark 1:14–15

Calling all to repent and believe in the Gospel, Jesus announces the arrival of God's Kingdom, as his teachings and miracles demonstrate God's mercy and love for all of us.

THE TRANSFIGURATION

We pray for a heart filled with hope.

Scripture: Matthew 17:1–13

Jesus takes Peter, James, and John up a mountain, where he is transfigured, shining with heavenly glory as he talks to Moses and Elijah, affirming his divinity and fulfillment of the Law and the Prophets.

THE INSTITUTION OF THE EUCHARIST

We pray for a heart filled with gratitude for the Holy Eucharist.

Scripture: Luke 22:14–23

On the night before his Crucifixion, Jesus shares the Last Supper with his Apostles, changing bread and wine into his Body, Blood, Soul, and Divinity as he institutes the Sacrament of the Holy Eucharist.

Sorrowful Mysteries

THE AGONY IN THE GARDEN

We pray for a contrite and obedient heart.

Scripture: Matthew 26:36–46

Jesus prays in the garden of Gethsemane before his arrest, demonstrating his profound obedience to the Father's will and revealing the depth of his human suffering.

THE SCOURGING AT THE PILLAR

We pray for a disciplined heart.

Scripture: Matthew 27:26

Jesus is brutally scourged and humiliated as he bears the weight of humanity's sins, proving his unconditional and sacrificial love for us.

THE CROWNING WITH THORNS

We pray for a detached heart.

Scripture: Matthew 27:27–31

Mocked and tortured by Roman soldiers, Jesus is crowned with thorns, and those who see him call for his crucifixion.

THE CARRYING OF THE CROSS

We pray for a patient heart.

Scripture: Matthew 27:32

Jesus carries the heavy Cross, showing his commitment to doing the Father's will as he endures suffering and humiliation on the path to Calvary.

THE CRUCIFIXION

We pray for a holy heart.

Scripture: Luke 23:33–46

Jesus, the Savior of the world, is nailed to the Cross and dies, offering himself with unconditional love and mercy for us as the ultimate sacrifice for our sins, while forgiving his persecutors and entrusting Mary and John to each other.

Glorious Mysteries

THE RESURRECTION

We pray for a faithful heart.

Scripture: Matthew 28:1–10

Jesus rises from the dead; he has defeated sin and death, offering hope and eternal life to all who believe in him.

THE ASCENSION

We pray for a heart ready for heaven.

Scripture: Luke 24:50–53

Telling his disciples to spread the Gospel and to baptize, Jesus ascends into heaven forty days after his Resurrection, returning to the Father.

THE DESCENT OF THE HOLY SPIRIT ON PENTECOST

We pray for a wise heart.

Scripture: Acts 2:1–13

As the Apostles are gathered in prayer with Mary, the Holy Spirit comes down upon them, strengthening them with gifts to proclaim the Gospel.

THE ASSUMPTION OF MARY

We pray for a heart devoted to Mary.

Scripture: Luke 1:46–56

Mary is taken body and soul into heaven by God's grace, affirming her unique role as the immaculate Mother of God and anticipating the resurrection of all believers at the end of time.

THE CORONATION OF MARY AS QUEEN OF HEAVEN AND EARTH

We pray for final perseverance of heart.

Scripture: Revelation 12:1–5

Mary is crowned Queen of Heaven and Earth by her son, Jesus Christ, as the exalted mother of the King.

How to
PRAY A
Better
ROSARY

Rosary Fundamentals

The Rosary is more than a prayer of words; it is a doorway to contemplation, inviting the soul to dwell upon the mysteries of the Faith. In the words of St. John Paul II, "to recite the Rosary is nothing other than to **contemplate with Mary the face of Christ**."[2]

The Rosary invites us not only to speak but also to ponder the lives of Christ and his mother. In the Rosary "we watch the mysteries of our Redemption as though they were unfolding before our eyes," Pope Leo XIII wrote. As St. John Paul II said, in the Rosary we "meditate on the mysteries of the Lord's life as seen through the eyes of her who was closest to the Lord."[3]

However, quiet contemplation of God does not come easily to most people, and we are often only taught the external aspects of the Rosary. These external aspects—the words of the prayers and the structure of the Rosary—are important. But sometimes we are not taught the fundamentals or shown how to lay a deep foundation for our prayer. Pope Leo XIII reminds us that "faith is exercised by vocally repeating the Our Father and Hail Mary of the Rosary prayers, or better still in the contemplation of the mysteries."[4]

Whether you're just getting started, persevering, or already committed to a daily Rosary, praying the Rosary

---

2. John Paul II, *Rosarium Virginis Mariae* (October 16, 2002), no. 3, vatican.va, emphasis added.
3. John Paul II, 12.
4. Leo XIII, *Adiutricem* (September 5, 1895), no. 25, vatican.va.

can actually be quite difficult. It can feel like trying to do a lot of things all at once. Sometimes it can feel as if praying the Rosary is like running a 5K while writing a short story while saying a specific number of Hail Marys over and over again.

Pope Benedict XVI said that praying the Rosary can be deeply fruitful as long as it is not done in a way that is just routine or "mechanical and superficial."[5] Yet, often we can find ourselves merely focused on getting to the end when we are praying the Rosary.

In the pages ahead we hope to give you the tools to learn the fundamentals and pray the Rosary in a much deeper way. We hope these tools will draw you into a closer encounter with Jesus and his Mother, Mary, as you raise your mind and heart to God.

St. John Paul II offers this advice: "The Rosary, precisely because it starts with Mary's own experience, is an exquisitely contemplative prayer. Without this contemplative dimension, it would lose its meaning." As we pray the Rosary, "the Christological and Marian meditation ... unfolds in the repetition of the *Hail Mary*."[6]

This booklet aims to present a method through which we can grow in contemplation of the prayers and mysteries of the Rosary.

---

5. Address of Pope Benedict XVI for the Recitation of the Holy Rosary at the Basilica of St. Mary Major on May 3, 2008, vatican.va.
6. John Paul II, *Rosarium Virginis Mariae*, 12, 32.

BUILDING PRAYER *"MUSCLES"*

In a way, learning to pray the Rosary can be compared to weight lifting. In the beginning, a personal trainer or coach will emphasize the importance of not sacrificing "form," or technique, for weight. This is because it is more important to lift with good form than to try to lift weights that are as heavy as possible. In the long run, learning and maintaining good form will allow an athlete to lift much more weight. In contrast, using momentum or other "cheats" to try to lift as much weight as possible may give the illusion of strength, but in the long run it may not build muscle well and can actually lead to injury.

While a weight lifter's goal is to build muscle, praying the Rosary is about raising our minds and hearts to God in prayer. The Rosary connects us to Our Lord and Our Lady as we reflect on how God has saved us and we ask Our Lady to pray for us.[7] No weight lifter could build muscle without weights, but "ego lifting," sacrificing good "form" to appear to be lifting more weight, may not achieve the goal of building muscle well. Similarly, we need to spend time in prayer, but repeating Hail Marys as fast as possible without knowing the fundamentals of how to meditate on the prayers and the mysteries of the Rosary may not help us achieve our goal of fruitful prayer.

To learn how to meditate while saying the words of the prayers—to learn good "form" for praying the Rosary—we'll focus on three aspects of the Rosary:

---

7. See *Rosarium Virginis Mariae*, 13, 16, and *Adiutricem*, 7, 25.

- first, the **persons** we speak to in the prayers,
- second, the words of the **prayers** themselves, and
- third, the **mysteries** of the Rosary.

We'll walk through each of these individually and provide a meditation exercise to begin building our prayer "muscles." Then, we'll take a look at what putting all three of these together while we pray the Rosary is like. In addition, this booklet introduces a prayer plan to help build prayer "muscles" in order to pray a more reflective Rosary and strengthen our relationship with God.

By learning the fundamentals, we hope to experience the motherhood of Mary and a personal encounter with Jesus in the Rosary and fall in love with this prayer.

From Repetition to Relationship

When learning the fundamentals of how to pray the Rosary in a way that connects us with Our Lord and Our Lady, we should first begin with the persons involved. When we pray the Rosary, we are lifting our minds and hearts to the Blessed Trinity: God the Father, the Son, and the Holy Spirit. We are also speaking to Mary, the Mother of God.

God is always present, and our prayer is always a response to his call to us. However, sometimes we can struggle with recognizing his presence, and it can feel as though we are alone or speaking to ourselves.

Meditating on Jesus' presence and Mary's gaze upon us will help us develop our awareness and remember that we are always in God's presence.

Most beautifully, our contemplation of God is two-sided; it is reciprocal. As we are praying the Rosary and offering our love to Jesus and Mary, we can remember that they too are looking upon us with love. In the Rosary we have the opportunity to look back upon Jesus and be aware of him who is always aware of us. Think of being with family members or friends who are sitting in the same room with us: they may not be speaking to us or even looking at us, but we still know they are present with us. This is the awareness that we are cultivating as we meditate on Jesus and Mary's love for us.

There are many ways we can tune our hearts to the presence of God and the gift of Mary's motherhood in our prayer of the Rosary. Here, we will be using a litany to assist us with our meditation.

The Litany of the Sacred Heart expresses a number of the characteristics of who Jesus is. Praying or simply reading through the Litany of the Sacred Heart can help us to look upon Jesus, to understand and value who he is and what it means to be in relationship with him. Praying or reading through the Litany of Loreto can help us encounter Our Lady in a similar way.

Now, we invite you to prayerfully read through the text of the Litany of the Sacred Heart on the following pages. Select some of the titles that speak most to you, and meditate upon what they mean and what they tell you about Jesus.

LITANY OF THE SACRED HEART

Lord, have mercy on us.

Christ, have mercy on us.

Lord, have mercy on us.

Christ, hear us.

Christ, graciously hear us.

God, the Father of Heaven, have mercy on us.

God, the Son, Redeemer of the world, have mercy on us.

God, the Holy Spirit, have mercy on us.

Holy Trinity, one God, have mercy on us.

Heart of Jesus, Son of the Eternal Father, have mercy on us.

Heart of Jesus, formed by the Holy Spirit in the womb of the Virgin Mother, have mercy on us.

Heart of Jesus, substantially united to the Word of God, have mercy on us.

Heart of Jesus, of infinite majesty, have mercy on us.

Heart of Jesus, sacred temple of God, have mercy on us.

Heart of Jesus, tabernacle of the Most High, have mercy on us.

Heart of Jesus, house of God and gate of heaven, have mercy on us.

Heart of Jesus, burning furnace of charity, have mercy on us.

Heart of Jesus, abode of justice and love, have mercy on us.

Heart of Jesus, full of goodness and love, have mercy on us.

Heart of Jesus, abyss of all virtues, have mercy on us.

Heart of Jesus, most worthy of all praise, have mercy on us.

Heart of Jesus, king and centre of all hearts, have mercy on us.

Heart of Jesus, in Whom are all the treasures of wisdom and knowledge, have mercy on us.

Heart of Jesus, in Whom dwells the fullness of divinity, have mercy on us.

Heart of Jesus, in Whom the Father was well pleased, have mercy on us.

Heart of Jesus, of Whose fullness we have all received, have mercy on us.

Heart of Jesus, desire of the everlasting hills, have mercy on us.

Heart of Jesus, patient and most merciful, have mercy on us.

Heart of Jesus, enriching all who invoke Thee, have mercy on us.

Heart of Jesus, fountain of life and holiness, have mercy on us.

Heart of Jesus, propitiation for our sins, have mercy on us.

Heart of Jesus, loaded down with opprobrium, have mercy on us.

Heart of Jesus, bruised for our offenses, have mercy on us.

Heart of Jesus, obedient unto death, have mercy on us.

Heart of Jesus, pierced with a lance, have mercy on us.

Heart of Jesus, source of all consolation, have mercy on us.

Heart of Jesus, our life and resurrection, have mercy on us.

Heart of Jesus, our peace and reconciliation, have mercy on us.

Heart of Jesus, victim for sin, have mercy on us.

Heart of Jesus, salvation of those who trust in Thee, have mercy on us.

Heart of Jesus, hope of those who die in Thee, have mercy on us.

Heart of Jesus, delight of all the saints, have mercy on us.

Lamb of God, Who takest away the sins of the world, spare us, O Lord.

Lamb of God, Who takest away the sins of the world, graciously hear us, O Lord.

Lamb of God, Who takest away the sins of the world, have mercy on us.

V. Jesus, meek and humble of Heart.

R. Make our hearts like unto Thine.

Let us pray:

O Almighty and eternal God, look upon the Heart of Thy dearly beloved Son, and upon the praise and satisfaction He offers Thee in the name of sinners and for those who seek Thy mercy; be Thou appeased, and grant us pardon in the name of the same Jesus Christ, Thy Son, Who liveth and reigneth with Thee, in the unity of the Holy Spirit forever and ever. Amen.[8]

---

8. From Charles J. Callan and John A. McHugh, *Blessed Be God: A Complete Catholic Prayer Book* (New York: P. J. Kenedy and Sons, 1925), archive.org/details/blessed-be-god-a-complete-catholic-prayer-book, capitalization and punctuation slightly revised and language slightly revised ("Holy Ghost" replaced with "Holy Spirit").

Meditate on Jesus with the Litany of the Sacred Heart

- Which of these titles in the Litany of the Sacred Heart resonates with you? Consider each title that stands out to you—what does this title mean?

- How do you see Jesus' presence in your life?

- Ask Jesus what he might want to tell you through his attributes expressed in the Litany of the Sacred Heart. Take just a moment to sit in silence with the Lord.

- Now, pray the first few prayers of the Rosary: 1 Our Father, 3 Hail Marys, and 1 Glory Be, and pray through these prayers slowly, focusing on the title of Jesus you have chosen. Allow your heart to speak directly to him through the words of the prayer, as you focus on the attributes of Jesus that most resonate with you. During this moment, ask him to give you the grace to recognize his presence and how he looks upon you with love as you look upon him.

LITANY OF LORETO

Lord, have mercy on us.

Christ, have mercy on us.

Lord, have mercy on us.

Christ, hear us.

Christ, graciously hear us.

God, the Father of heaven, have mercy on us.

God, the Son, Redeemer of the world, have mercy on us.

God, the Holy Spirit, have mercy on us.

Holy Trinity, one God, have mercy on us.

Holy Mary, pray for us.

Holy Mother of God, pray for us.

Holy Virgin of virgins, pray for us.

Mother of Christ, pray for us.

Mother of the Church, pray for us.

Mother of Mercy, pray for us.

Mother of divine grace, pray for us.

Mother most pure, pray for us.

Mother most chaste, pray for us.

Mother inviolate, pray for us.

Mother undefiled, pray for us.

Mother most amiable, pray for us.

Mother admirable, pray for us.

Mother of good counsel, pray for us.

Mother of our Creator, pray for us.

Mother of our Saviour, pray for us.

Virgin most prudent, pray for us.

Virgin most venerable, pray for us.

Virgin most renowned, pray for us.

Virgin most powerful, pray for us.

Virgin most merciful, pray for us.

Virgin most faithful, pray for us.

Mirror of justice, pray for us.

Seat of wisdom, pray for us.

Cause of our joy, pray for us.

Spiritual vessel, pray for us.

Vessel of honour, pray for us.

Singular vessel of devotion, pray for us.

Mystical rose, pray for us.

Tower of David, pray for us.

Tower of ivory, pray for us.

House of gold, pray for us.

Ark of the covenant, pray for us.

Gate of heaven, pray for us.

Morning star, pray for us.

Health of the sick, pray for us.

Refuge of sinners, pray for us.

Solace of Migrants, pray for us.

Comfort of the afflicted, pray for us.

Help of Christians, pray for us.

Queen of Angels, pray for us.

Queen of Patriarchs, pray for us.

Queen of Prophets, pray for us.

Queen of Apostles, pray for us.

Queen of Martyrs, pray for us.

Queen of Confessors, pray for us.

Queen of Virgins, pray for us.

Queen of all Saints, pray for us.

Queen conceived without original sin, pray for us.

Queen assumed into heaven, pray for us.

Queen of the most holy Rosary, pray for us.

Queen of families, pray for us.

Queen of peace, pray for us.

Lamb of God, Who takes away the sins of the world, spare us, O Lord.

Lamb of God, Who takes away the sins of the world, graciously hear us, O Lord.

Lamb of God, Who takes away the sins of the world, have mercy on us.

Pray for us, O holy Mother of God.

That we may be made worthy of the promises of Christ.

Let us pray.

Grant, we beseech thee,

O Lord God,

That we, your servants,

May enjoy perpetual health of mind and body;

And by the glorious intercession of the Blessed Mary, ever Virgin, may be delivered from present sorrow, and obtain eternal joy.

Through Christ our Lord.

Amen.[9]

---

9. "The Litany of Loreto," "The Holy Rosary," vatican.va, accessed August 26, 2024, https://www.vatican.va/special/rosary/documents/litanie-lauretane_en.html.

Biblical Roots of the Rosary

The prayers of the Rosary are all rooted in Scripture, the Word of God. As we continue learning the fundamentals of how to pray the Rosary in a way that connects us with Our Lord and Our Lady, the words of the prayers we say can be another fruitful source of meditation.

The Our Father comes directly from the Gospel of Matthew, where we read that Jesus taught his disciples to pray. The Hail Mary comes from the Church's tradition of using words of Scripture to pray more deeply, like a little *lectio divina*, or "divine reading."

The *Catechism of the Catholic Church* explains the biblical roots of the Hail Mary:

> The greeting of the angel Gabriel opens this prayer. It is God himself who, through his angel as intermediary, greets Mary. Our prayer dares to take up this greeting to Mary with the regard God had for the lowliness of his humble servant and to exult in the joy he finds in her ... *Blessed art thou among women and blessed is the fruit of thy womb, Jesus.* After the angel's greeting, we make Elizabeth's greeting our own. (CCC 2676)

In this way, the words of the Hail Mary lead us to sit with Mary and speak with her. The prayers of the Rosary create space for contemplation and allow us to listen to Mary tell us the story of her son's life. As the *Catechism* says,

> Mary is the perfect *Orans* (pray-er), a figure of the Church. When we pray to her, we are adhering with her to the plan of the Father, who sends his Son to save all men. Like the beloved disciple we welcome Jesus' mother into our homes, for she has become the mother of all the living. We can pray with and to her. (CCC 2679)

Our Blessed Mother never tires of hearing us say, "I love you," and there is no better way to say that than by praying the Rosary. The *Catechism* goes on to say,

> Because of Mary's singular cooperation with the action of the Holy Spirit, the Church loves to pray in communion with the Virgin Mary, to magnify with her the great things the Lord has done for her, and to entrust supplications and praises to her. (CCC 2682)

THE ROSARY PRAYERS IN SCRIPTURE

The following chart shows some of the biblical roots of the Our Father, the Hail Mary, and the Glory Be for you to use in your own prayer of the Rosary. Some Scripture verses give us the words we pray, while other verses form the foundation for the prayers. Any of these prayers can be used for meditation on God's Word while we pray the Rosary.

To help your meditation, you can look up the verses in the Bible to read the surrounding passages for context, or you can simply slowly read through the words of the prayers, focusing on what they mean, what you are saying to God, and what God might be saying to you.

Our Father

Note: Matthew 6:9–13 gives us the exact words of the Our Father.

THE PRAYER	SCRIPTURE
Our Father who art in heaven, hallowed be thy name.	Ezekiel 36:23: "And I will vindicate the holiness of my great name, which has been profaned among the nations, and which you have profaned among them; and the nations will know that I am the LORD, says the Lord GOD, when through you I vindicate my holiness before their eyes."
Thy kingdom come. Thy will be done on earth, as it is in heaven.	Matthew 6:33: "But seek first his kingdom and his righteousness, and all these things shall be yours as well."
Give us this day our daily bread,	Matthew 6:25: "Therefore I tell you, do not be anxious about your life, what you shall eat or what you shall drink, nor about your body, what you shall put on. Is not life more than food, and the body more than clothing?"
	John 6:51: "I am the living bread which came down from heaven; if any one eats of this bread, he will live for ever; and the bread which I shall give for the life of the world is my flesh."
and forgive us our trespasses, as we forgive those who trespass against us,	Matthew 6:14: "For if you forgive men their trespasses, your heavenly Father also will forgive you; but if you do not forgive men their trespasses, neither will your Father forgive your trespasses."
and lead us not into temptation, but deliver us from evil.	James 1:13–14: "Let no one say when he is tempted, 'I am tempted by God'; for God cannot be tempted with evil and he himself tempts no one; but each person is tempted when he is lured and enticed by his own desire."

Hail Mary

THE PRAYER	SCRIPTURE
Hail Mary, full of grace, the Lord is with thee.	Luke 1:28: "And he [the angel Gabriel] came to her and said, 'Hail, full of grace, the Lord is with you!'"
Blessed art thou among women, and blessed is the fruit of thy womb, Jesus.	Luke 1:42: "And she [Elizabeth] exclaimed with a loud cry, 'Blessed are you among women, and blessed is the fruit of your womb!'"
	Luke 1:48: "For he has regarded the low estate of his handmaiden. For behold, henceforth all generations will call me blessed."
Holy Mary, Mother of God,	Luke 1:43: "And why is this granted me, that the mother of my Lord should come to me?"
	Matthew 1:23 (see Isaiah 7:14): "'Behold, a virgin shall conceive and bear a son, and his name shall be called Emmanuel' (which means, God with us)."
pray for us sinners, now and at the hour of our death. Amen.	John 19:26–27: "When Jesus saw his mother, and the disciple whom he loved standing near, he said to his mother, 'Woman, behold, your son!' Then he said to the disciple, 'Behold, your mother!' And from that hour the disciple took her to his own home."

Glory Be

THE PRAYER	SCRIPTURE
Glory be to the Father, and to the Son, and to the Holy Spirit,	Romans 11:36: "For from him and through him and to him are all things. To him be glory for ever. Amen."
as it was in the beginning, is now, and ever shall be, world without end. Amen.	Revelation 1:8: "'I am the Alpha and the Omega,' says the Lord God, who is and who was and who is to come, the Almighty."

Meditate on the Words of the Hail Mary in Scripture

- Slowly pray each line of the Hail Mary, and reflect on the Scripture verse that is its foundation.

- Start with the words spoken to Mary at the Annunciation, recalling what God has done for Mary and what he has done in salvation history through Mary to bring us Jesus.

- Then consider the words of Elizabeth to Mary at another pivotal moment in salvation history, in which Mary goes out of herself and brings the gift of Jesus to Elizabeth and by extension to all of us.

- Now recall the name of Jesus, which forms the center of the prayer.

- Finally, ask Our Lady to pray for us at the two most important times in our life: now, because we only have the present moment, and at the hour of our death, the pivotal moment when Our Lady can comfort and protect us.

- Now, we invite you to slowly pray the first few prayers of the Rosary: 1 Our Father, 3 Hail Marys, and 1 Glory Be.

The Mysteries of the Rosary in Scripture

The Rosary invites us to reflect upon the events in the lives of Our Lord and Our Lady that we typically refer to as the mysteries of the Rosary. Like the prayers of the Rosary, the mysteries are biblically rooted, derived from pivotal moments in the lives of Jesus and Mary. Through these mysteries, the Rosary brings us to ponder each day the foundational truths of our Faith. Meditating on the mysteries is a fundamental element of praying the Rosary in a way that connects us with Our Lord and Our Lady.

When we consider the mysteries of the Rosary, perhaps the word "mystery" stands out to us. We may have heard the narratives of the mysteries of the Rosary before, but their nature as "mysteries" means that their contemplative fruit is inexhaustible. There is always something new Jesus can share with us through the mysteries of the Rosary and always more that we can reflect upon in our meditation upon the events of Jesus' and Mary's lives.

As we begin to meditate more deeply on the mysteries of the Rosary, it can be helpful to start slowly. Instead of jumping into the full Rosary and trying to meditate on five mysteries in one sitting, build up gradually.

Pick one mystery and set aside time to focus your whole prayer time on reflecting on the moment in Scripture it contains.

To aid your meditation, you can use a form of prayer such as *lectio divina* or "divine reading." Begin by reading through the Scripture associated with that mystery, listed in the chart below, then reflect on the Scripture passage prayerfully.

The more we concentrate on prayerfully reading about the mysteries, asking Jesus to reveal himself to us through these moments of his life and asking for the grace to acknowledge God's presence with us, the more we will be moved with greater ease to meditate on these mysteries as we are invited to do in the Rosary.

THE ANNUNCIATION	Luke 1:26–38
THE VISITATION	Luke 1:39–56
THE NATIVITY	Luke 2:1–20
THE PRESENTATION OF JESUS IN THE TEMPLE	Luke 2:22–39
THE FINDING OF JESUS IN THE TEMPLE	Luke 2:41–52
THE BAPTISM OF JESUS	Matthew 3:13–17
THE WEDDING AT CANA	John 2:1–12
THE PROCLAMATION OF THE KINGDOM AND THE CALL TO CONVERSION	Mark 1:14–15
THE TRANSFIGURATION	Matthew 17:1–13
THE INSTITUTION OF THE EUCHARIST	Luke 22:14–23

THE AGONY IN THE GARDEN	Matthew 26:36–46
THE SCOURGING AT THE PILLAR	Matthew 27:26
THE CROWNING WITH THORNS	Matthew 27:27–31
THE CARRYING OF THE CROSS	Matthew 27:32
THE CRUCIFIXION	Luke 23:33–46

THE RESURRECTION	Matthew 28:1–10
THE ASCENSION	Luke 24:50–53
THE DESCENT OF THE HOLY SPIRIT ON PENTECOST	Acts 2:1–13
THE ASSUMPTION OF MARY	Luke 1:46–56
THE CORONATION OF MARY AS QUEEN OF HEAVEN AND EARTH	Revelation 12:1–5

Meditate on the Mysteries of the Rosary Through Scripture

- Choose one of the mysteries of the Rosary. Look up the Scripture passage associated with it.

- First, read the Scripture for its narrative, the story it presents. You may know the story already, but whether this is your first time or hundredth time encountering this moment in Jesus' life, read slowly and carefully, maybe even out loud. What is happening in this passage? Is this a joyful moment, like the Visitation, in which Mary and Elizabeth greet each other with love? Is this an illuminating moment, like the Baptism of the Lord, in which we see Jesus' divinity? Is this a sorrowful moment, as in the Carrying of the Cross, where we see Christ's love for us through his sacrifice? Is it a glorious moment, such as the Resurrection, where we see the culmination of salvation history and our redemption? All of the mysteries have their own unique space in salvation history, the story of God's love for us. Read through the Scripture passage to learn the story or refresh your memory of the narrative.

- Next, read the Scripture again, but this time let your heart and mind respond to God's Word. What could God be saying to you personally through this passage? Maybe a specific word or phrase stands out to you. If so, let this reverberate in your mind. If you like to journal, now is a great time to write down your thoughts on the passage and consider how God might be speaking to you through his Word.

- Third, bring your thoughts to God in verbal prayer. Put your feelings and thoughts into words or a mental image, and speak to God, either out loud or silently in your heart. Ask yourself what your heart is moved to say. Do you feel moved to thanksgiving or to praise God for his goodness? Do you feel moved to ask for grace or redemption? Do you feel moved to just sit silently with the Lord? Bring all of this to him at this moment.

- Finally, this prayer leads us to contemplation. There is no formula for contemplation, as it is a gift from God. Instead, we dispose ourselves to experience the presence of God. In this moment, spend some time gazing at the Lord and simply be with him. Whether or not you experience a feeling of his presence, know that Jesus desires to spend time with you and is gazing upon you with love.

- After spending time in meditation on the mystery you have chosen, we invite you to slowly pray the first few prayers of the Rosary: 1 Our Father, 3 Hail Marys, and 1 Glory Be. As you pray through these prayers, focus not on the words this time but instead on the mystery you have just spent time meditating on. The goal is to enter deeply into these mysteries and build up your relationship with Jesus and Mary in the process.

Putting It All Together

Now that we have explored and practiced three methods of meditation that can be integrated into the Rosary for a deeper encounter with the Lord, we can begin a "slow build" to praying the Rosary in a way that deeply connects us to Our Lord and Our Lady.

We will build up from the first few prayers of the Rosary, choosing one mystery to focus on at a time, to a full Rosary, in which we experience the "contemplative dimension" that St. John Paul II says is so integral to the prayer of the Rosary.

If you're already praying a Rosary a day, maybe two or three times a day, that's wonderful! We encourage you to continue praying the Rosary and begin to incorporate these methods of meditation into your daily Rosary. However, if you're not praying a Rosary a day and would like to, or you want to deepen your experience of the Rosary, we encourage you to try this slow build. Start with the fundamentals and immerse yourself in the Word of God as you pray.

This slow build takes into account our humanity and how we grow. As in the weight lifting analogy from earlier, we are looking to start with the fundamentals to build good Rosary "form" and develop prayer "muscles"! We will then be equipped to make the Rosary a regular part of our spiritual lives and our prayer for the rest of our lives.

A "SLOW BUILD"

BEGIN
Begin with just the first few prayers of the Rosary, as you have in the sections above. Don't rush yourself to say 50 Hail Marys in one sitting. Instead, set aside five, ten, or fifteen minutes. Choose one prayer, one mystery, or one attribute of Jesus or Mary to focus on during that prayer time. Then pray 1 Our Father, 3 Hail Marys, and 1 Glory Be. The next day, choose another mystery, and do the same. Read the Scriptures and use the *lectio divina* method to really concentrate on using the prayers to meditate on the lives of Christ and Mary. Slowly work on building up your prayer "muscles" and your awareness of the presence of God as you pray.

BUILD UP
As you become more and more comfortable with meditating as you pray, move from the first few prayers to saying a full decade of the Rosary (1 Our Father, 10 Hail Marys, and 1 Glory Be), meditating on a single mystery. Take a few weeks, saying one decade a day, focusing on one mystery at a time, to work through all the mysteries.

As you build your capacity, perhaps look up some commentaries or reflections on the mysteries, or sacred art depicting them, to lead you more deeply into their meaning. This process is not only developing your capacity to pray but is also intentionally building an inner "library" or "archive" of sources of meditation you can pull from as you are praying the

Rosary. The more you return to the Scriptures, reflections or commentaries on the life of Christ, or sacred art that resonates with you, the more you will be able to meditate independently on the mysteries of the Rosary as you pray.

As we have real prayerful encounters with the Gospels, as we receive and drink of the insights of the saints, as we visualize and ponder the beauty of the artwork, then it will be much more natural for our minds and hearts to contemplate the mysteries. We will be moved with greater ease to meditate on these mysteries as we are invited to do in the Rosary.

CONTINUE
Build up to two decades a day. Continue to increase the number of decades slowly, moving at your own pace. Remember that you are in the presence of God; meditate on his love for you as you gaze upon him and spend time with him in prayer.

DON'T STOP!
Continue to build until you are praying a full Rosary and spending that time lifting your mind and heart to God. With the foundation you have laid and the prayer "muscles" you have been exercising, you will build your capacity to pray more deeply and spontaneously so that the Rosary can connect you more and more with Our Lord and Our Lady, even as you are going about daily tasks.

A Prayer **PLAN**

The Rosary in a Year Prayer Plan

To help provide a structure, Ascension has developed *The Rosary in a Year* Prayer Plan. This plan lays out a method to pray a better Rosary in 365 days, taking the skills you have learned in this booklet and offering them in a structured way that you can use to turn a Rosary that feels repetitive into a Rosary that develops your relationship with Jesus and Mary over a year.

The Rosary in a Year Prayer Plan will tell you which prayers to pray each day and which Bible verses or mysteries to meditate on. It even includes information about additional reflections and sacred art you can find and use for your own meditation. This content is organized into six phases to help you slowly build a better Rosary.

You'll begin by developing awareness of Jesus and Mary, learning the biblical roots of the Rosary, and meditating on the narratives of the mysteries of the Rosary, then move to deeper meditation through *lectio* and *visio divina*, and finally be able to meditate throughout the full Rosary on your own. In the next section of this booklet, you will find a full outline of these six phases that compose the overall structure of *The Rosary in a Year* Prayer Plan.

Visit Ascensionpress.com/rosaryinayear to download *The Rosary in a Year* Prayer Plan and start praying a better Rosary today!

Pray with Us

Are you interested in following *The Rosary in a Year* Prayer Plan with us? Fr. Mark-Mary Ames, CFR, will be following *The Rosary in a Year* Prayer Plan in *The Rosary in a Year (with Fr. Mark-Mary Ames)* podcast beginning January 1, 2025. Join him as he reads through the Scriptures, reflections from saints on the mysteries, and meditation prompts for sacred art, and prays each day, following the Prayer Plan! You can begin on January 1, 2025, or follow along with the podcast at any time after that.

If you have journeyed through the Bible with us by listening to the chart-topping podcast *The Bible in a Year (with Fr. Mike Schmitz)*™ featuring Jeff Cavins, you will love discovering the connections between the Rosary and the Bible! Though many Catholics are unaware of it, this Marian prayer is steeped in Scripture. Throughout the course of this year, you will encounter its biblical roots.

Similarly, if you encountered the *Catechism* with us by listening to *The Catechism in a Year*™ *(with Fr. Mike Schmitz)* podcast, you know the importance of meditative prayer and contemplating the life of Christ.

Whether or not you have listened to these podcasts and are familiar with Scripture or the *Catechism*, in this *Rosary in a Year* podcast, you will find a new (or should we say centuries old!) way of meditating on significant moments in the lives of our Lord Jesus Christ and his mother. As the *Catechism* states, "Prayer is the encounter of God's thirst with ours" (CCC 2560).

In the coming year, you will experience 365 days dedicated to growing in prayer with the Lord.

The Rosary in a Year podcast will guide listeners through six phases, doing a "slow build" to form a lasting habit of prayer and gain the tools to enter more deeply into fruitful meditation on the lives of Jesus and Mary through the Rosary. We will be equipped to pray the Rosary with fervor, putting Christ first in our lives as we still ourselves to drink deeply of the truth of God's life and love.

GOALS FOR EACH PHASE

Phase 1 (Days 1–7)
FORMING THE RELATIONSHIP

In this phase, we will deepen our relationships with Jesus and Mary, the two persons we primarily meditate on in the mysteries of the Rosary. To accomplish this, we will practice awareness of the fact that we truly are praying in the presence of Jesus and Mary. Then, we will reflect on some of the titles of Mary and Jesus found in the Litany of the Blessed Virgin (the Litany of Loreto) and the Litany of the Sacred Heart. There's no need to pray the litanies in full right now—we will just select one or two titles to reflect on.

We will also begin to incorporate the prayers of the Rosary into our daily lives. To accomplish this goal, we will pray a short, manageable set of prayers each day: 1 Our Father, 3 Hail Marys, and 1 Glory Be.

By the end of this phase, you will have begun building the mental muscle of focus needed for prayer by praying a short selection of the prayers of the Rosary daily, and you will have a new way to deepen your relationships with Jesus and Mary!

We will pray 1 Our Father, 3 Hail Marys, and 1 Glory Be each day.

Phase 2 (Days 8–68)
BIBLICAL ROOTS OF THE ROSARY

In this phase we will learn about the biblical roots of the prayers and the mysteries of the Rosary.

Understanding the deep spiritual meaning of the Rosary is essential if we are going to still ourselves and drink deeply of the truth of the life and love of God through this prayer. In this second phase of *The Rosary in a Year*, the focus will be on understanding the biblical basis of the prayers and mysteries of the Rosary.

First, on Days 8–28, we will delve into the biblical roots of the prayers of the Rosary. The Our Father is found in Scripture word for word, while other prayers like the Hail Mary and Hail, Holy Queen are not. But every single prayer of the Rosary has biblical roots that we will uncover in the coming days.

Second, on Days 29–68, we will discover the biblical roots of the mysteries of the Rosary. Each mystery of the Rosary is a chance to meditate on a significant event in the lives of Jesus and Mary. In this phase, we will read, and re-read, a Scripture passage related to each of these events.

By the end of this phase, you will understand the biblical foundations of each prayer of the Rosary, as well as each of the twenty mysteries of the Rosary. This is a chance to make the basic elements of the Rosary, the prayers and the mysteries, more full of meaning in your prayer life!

We will continue to pray 1 Our Father, 3 Hail Marys, and 1 Glory Be each day.

Phase 3 (Days 69–188)
MEDITATING ON THE MYSTERIES

There are many ways to meditate on the mysteries of the Rosary. In this phase, we will experience three:

- reading Scripture prayerfully (*lectio divina*),
- reading reflections from the saints and others, and
- viewing sacred art prayerfully ("*visio divina*").

In addition to practicing meditation in these various ways, we will increase our time commitment by beginning to pray one decade of the Rosary each day.

First, on Days 69–88, we will meditate on each mystery of the Rosary by praying with the Scriptures associated with it. Unlike last time, when we were reading the Scriptures primarily to understand the *narrative* behind the mystery, this time we are praying with the Scriptures in order to meditate. This form of prayer is traditionally known as *lectio divina*.

Second, on Days 89–128, we will meditate on each mystery by prayerfully reading two reflections, mostly from the saints, on that mystery. There are so many riches and insights to glean from the great saints who came before us!

Third, on Days 129–188, we will meditate on each mystery by prayerfully contemplating three different images. Each of the images is a beautiful piece of sacred art that can lead the viewer into a deeper understanding of the mystery of the Rosary it depicts. This form of prayer is sometimes called *"visio divina."*

By the end of this phase, you will have meditated on the Scriptures, prayerfully read reflections from the saints, and prayed with sacred images depicting each mystery of the Rosary. You will have a true interior "library" or "archive" of phrases, insights, and imagery for each mystery of the Rosary!

We will pray 1 decade of the Rosary (1 Our Father, 10 Hail Marys, and 1 Glory Be) each day.

Phase 4 (Days 189–208)
FINDING FOCUS

Now that we have practiced many ways of meditating on the mysteries of the Rosary, it's time to enter into prayer without new materials. In this phase, we will independently meditate on each mystery for 10 minutes each day, drawing on our inner "library" or "archive" of knowledge, insight, and images that we have built up over the last phase. You may find a journal to be a helpful tool.

With the foundation we have laid and the prayer "muscles" we are exercising, we are building our capacity to pray more deeply and spontaneously so that the Rosary can connect us more and more with Our Lord and Our Lady, even as we are going about daily tasks.

By the end of this phase, you will have practiced independent meditation on each mystery of the Rosary. You will be prepared to meditate more naturally while praying a full Rosary in the days to come!

We will pray 1 decade of the Rosary (1 Our Father, 10 Hail Marys, and 1 Glory Be) each day.

Phase 5 (Days 209-335)
BUILDING UP THE DECADES

In this phase, we will continue drawing on our inner "library" or "archive" each day to meditate while praying the prayers of the Rosary.

We will build up the number of decades prayed each day, from 2 decades up to 5 decades each day.

Phase 6 (Days 336–365)
PRAYING TOGETHER

In this final phase, *we will pray a daily Rosary, meditating on the mysteries of the day,* using the prayer "muscles" we have built during this year.

AND BEYOND …

After the podcast ends, we will be equipped with tools and skills to *pray,* not just *say,* the Rosary devoutly each day as we seek to grow closer to Christ through his Mother.